THE
NBA
A HISTORY OF HOOPS

Published by Creative Education
P.O. Box 227, Mankato, Minnesota 56002
Creative Education is an imprint of The Creative Company
www.thecreativecompany.us

Design and production by Christine Vanderbeek
Art direction by Rita Marshall

Printed by Corporate Graphics in the United States of America

Photographs by Dreamstime (Munktcu), Getty Images (Randy Belice/NBAE, John Biever/Sports Illustrated, Andrew D. Bernstein/NBAE, Michael Bradley, Nathaniel S. Butler/NBAE, Focus on Sport, John Iacono/Sports Illustrated, Adam Jones, Heinz Kluetmeier/Sports Illustrated, Fernando Medina/NBAE, Manny Millan/Sports Illustrated, Layne Murdoch/NBAE, Joe Murphy/NBAE, Paul Natkin/WireImage, NBA Photos/NBAE, Scott Olson, Dick Raphael/NBAE, SM/AIUEO, Rick Stewart), iStockphoto (Brandon Laufenberg)

Library of Congress Cataloging-in-Publication Data
Caffrey, Scott.
The story of the Chicago Bulls / by Scott Caffrey.
p. cm. — (The NBA: a history of hoops)
Includes index.
Summary: The history of the Chicago Bulls professional basketball team from its start in 1966 to today, spotlighting the franchise's greatest players and reliving its most dramatic moments.
ISBN 978-1-58341-939-7
1. Chicago Bulls (Basketball team)—History—Juvenile literature.
I. Title. II. Series.
GV885.52.C45C34 2010   796.323'640977311—dc22   2009034779

CPSIA: 120109 PO1093

First Edition
2 4 6 8 9 7 5 3 1

Page 3: Forward Luol Deng
Pages 4–5: Pregame at Chicago's United Center

THE STORY OF THE

CHICAGO
BULLS

SCOTT CAFFREY

CREATIVE EDUCATION

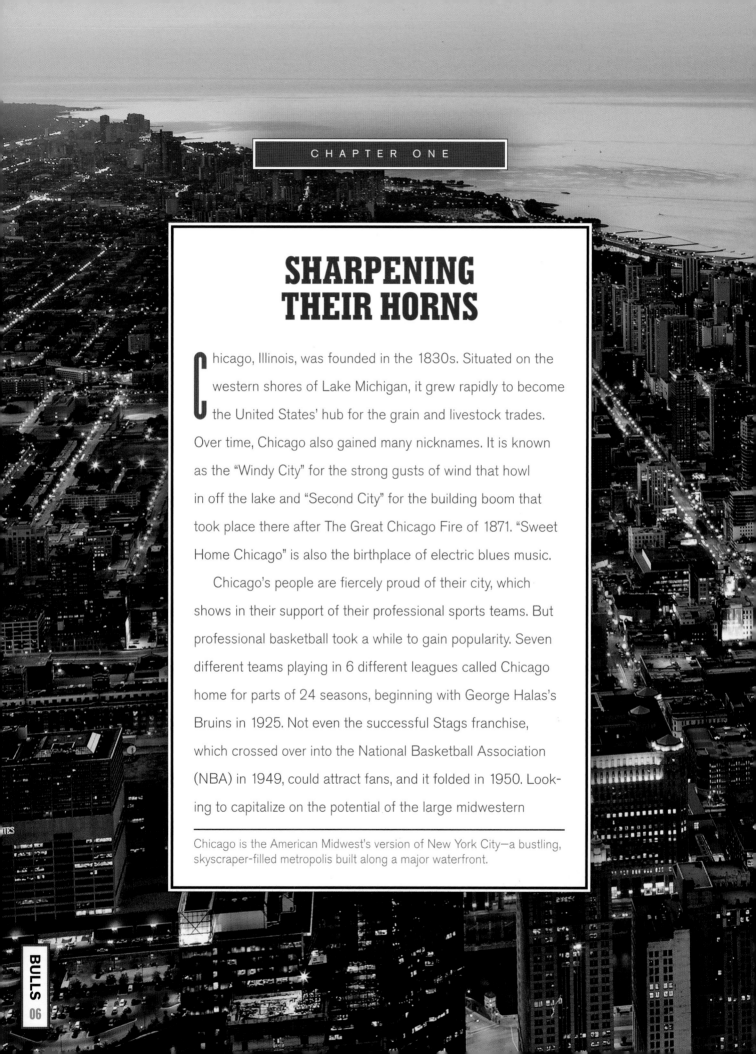

CHAPTER ONE

SHARPENING THEIR HORNS

Chicago, Illinois, was founded in the 1830s. Situated on the western shores of Lake Michigan, it grew rapidly to become the United States' hub for the grain and livestock trades. Over time, Chicago also gained many nicknames. It is known as the "Windy City" for the strong gusts of wind that howl in off the lake and "Second City" for the building boom that took place there after The Great Chicago Fire of 1871. "Sweet Home Chicago" is also the birthplace of electric blues music.

Chicago's people are fiercely proud of their city, which shows in their support of their professional sports teams. But professional basketball took a while to gain popularity. Seven different teams playing in 6 different leagues called Chicago home for parts of 24 seasons, beginning with George Halas's Bruins in 1925. Not even the successful Stags franchise, which crossed over into the National Basketball Association (NBA) in 1949, could attract fans, and it folded in 1950. Looking to capitalize on the potential of the large midwestern

Chicago is the American Midwest's version of New York City—a bustling, skyscraper-filled metropolis built along a major waterfront.

market, the NBA granted Chicago another franchise in 1966. Given the city's long history as a cattle town, coming up with the new team's name was easy: "Bulls" would symbolize the strength, size, and powerful will of Chicago's latest addition.

While most expansion teams have a hard time winning, the 1966–67 Chicago Bulls were different. Under head coach Johnny "Red" Kerr, who grew up in Chicago and was a basketball star at local Tilden Technical High School and at the University of Illinois, the club went 33–48 and made it into the playoffs. It was an NBA first for an expansion team, and it earned Kerr Coach of the Year honors. Rookie center Erwin Mueller was selected to the NBA All-Rookie team, and playmaking guard Guy Rodgers tallied a league-leading 908 assists. But the team couldn't sustain its success the next season. The Bulls

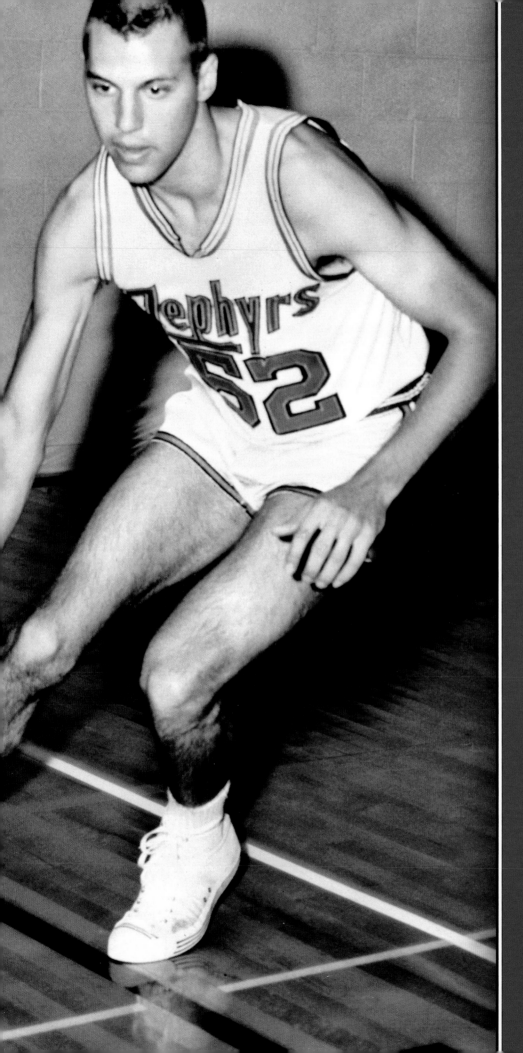

IT TOOK A WHILE FOR PROFESSIONAL BASKETBALL TO CATCH ON IN CHICAGO. The Stags franchise took the court in 1946 and played three seasons in the Basketball Association of America (BAA) and one final season in the new NBA in 1949. Under future Hall of Fame coach Harold Olsen, the Stags got off to a quick start, advancing to the league finals in their inaugural season but losing to the Philadelphia Warriors. Despite making it to the playoffs every season and compiling an impressive 145–92 record, the team failed to win over fans. "Pro basketball was fairly new at the time," said point guard Mickey Rottner. "It didn't catch on the way we all hoped it would." Following the 1949–50 season, the Stags disbanded. In 1961, the Chicago Packers arrived, but they changed their name to the Zephyrs the next year and moved to Baltimore in 1963 to become the Bullets. Finally, in 1966, the NBA granted Chicago another franchise, the Bulls. In tribute to their predecessors, the Bulls wore replicas of the 1946 Stags uniforms three times during the 2005–06 season.

DURING HIS DECADE-LONG PLAY-
ING CAREER, JERRY SLOAN WAS
THE KIND OF PLAYER WHO SIMPLY
WORKED HARDER THAN MOST
OTHERS ON THE COURT. Sloan, "The
Original Bull," was Chicago's first-ever
draft pick in the NBA's 1966 expansion
draft. And from the minute he stepped
onto the floor, Bulls fans came to revere
him for his unparalleled toughness and
grit. As Sloan humbly explained, "I had
to do whatever I could to play. I couldn't
compete with [other players] athleti-
cally." Although the playing phase of his
career was cut short in 1976 due to a
knee injury, perseverance became his
trademark. The next year, Sloan entered
into Chicago's coaching ranks as an
assistant and was then elevated to
head coach in 1979. But after compiling a losing record (94–121) over nearly
three seasons, Sloan's coaching career
in Chicago ended midway through a
terrible 1981–82 season. He experi-
enced greater coaching success with
the Utah Jazz. As of 2010, Sloan was
the only coach in NBA history to record
1,000 wins with 1 franchise (Utah) and
had coached 1 team longer than anyone else in league history as well.

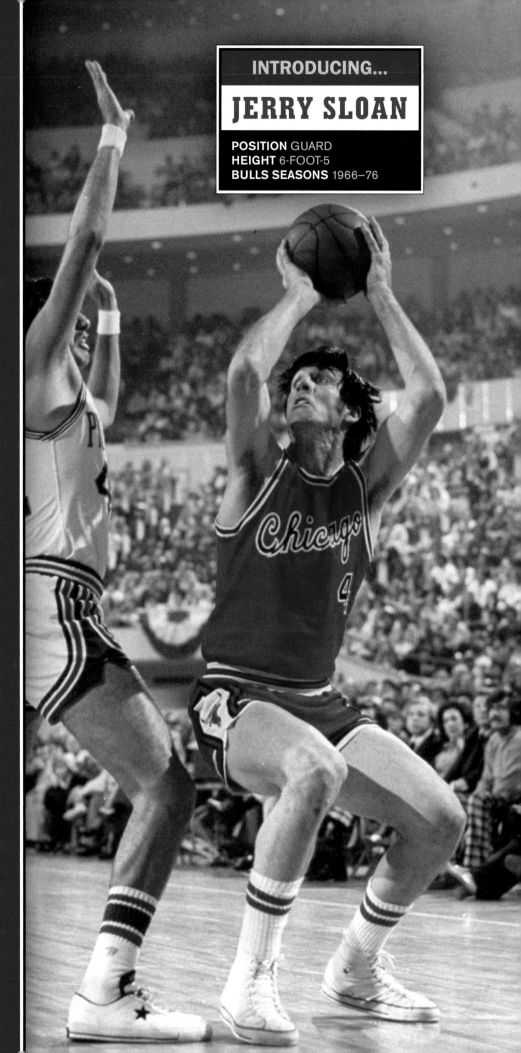

INTRODUCING...

JERRY SLOAN

POSITION GUARD
HEIGHT 6-FOOT-5
BULLS SEASONS 1966–76

took a step backward with only 29 wins, and Kerr resigned.

Although the first two seasons under new coach Dick Motta weren't pretty, Chicago's record improved. By 1970–71, the Bulls had soared to second place in the Western Conference's newly formed Midwest Division with a 51–31 record. Motta was named NBA Coach of the Year and then helped Chicago reel off 3 more seasons of 50 or more wins. But despite such regular-season success, the Bulls were no match for conference rivals such as the Los Angeles Lakers in the postseason.

By the 1972–73 season, the Bulls had built a starting lineup that included scrappy point guard Norm Van Lier and hulking, seven-foot center Tom Boerwinkle. The team also featured combative guard Jerry Sloan, a budding star who was selected to the NBA All-Defensive team six times in seven years. The offensive punch in this defensive powerhouse came courtesy of forwards Chet Walker and Bob Love. "Playing the Bulls is like running through a barbed wire fence," said Lakers guard Gail Goodrich. "You may win the game, but they're gonna put lumps on you."

huge drop in the team's performance in 1975–76 cost Motta his job. New coach Ed Badger took over for the 1976–77 season, the same year the team acquired center Artis Gilmore, a player known as "The A-Train" because of his enormous size and strength. That year, Gilmore led the team in scoring and rebounding and remade the Bulls into a winner. Despite Gilmore's consistently impressive numbers, a championship eluded him during his six seasons with the team. Following the 1981–82 season, the Bulls decided to rebuild with younger players, and Gilmore was traded to the San Antonio Spurs. "It's a shame we couldn't put a better team around Artis," noted Van Lier. "He did everything he could, but when we lost, he always got the blame."

Despite the rebuilding efforts, Chicago was in disarray. Between 1976 and 1982, the team had hired and fired six coaches, including former fan favorite Sloan. Standouts such as guard Reggie Theus and forward Orlando Woolridge provided steady play in the early 1980s, but the Bulls lacked competitiveness. Fortunately, a huge gust of Air was on the way to help turn the team's fortunes around.

INTRODUCING...

BOB LOVE

POSITION FORWARD
HEIGHT 6-FOOT-8
BULLS SEASONS 1968–77

FOR SOME PEOPLE, STUTTERING CAN BE A BIG PROBLEM. For Bob Love, it meant the difference between silence and speech. While Love was a smooth player on the court, leading the Bulls in scoring for seven straight seasons, he was dragged down by what he considered to be an embarrassing stuttering problem off the court. "Butterbean," as Love was known while growing up in Louisiana, would get so flustered when he tried to talk that he often chose to be silent to avoid ridicule. Finally, at age 45, he decided to conquer his problem, attacking it the same way he approached basketball: he practiced. Today, Love is a motivational speaker who talks eloquently in front of large crowds. Making more than 300 appearances a year, Love has become the Bulls' "goodwill ambassador," representing the organization throughout Chicago. "Don't give up, and always try to do your best," Love said. "If you take the first step, someone will help you take the next one." To honor Love's efforts, the Bulls retired his number 10 jersey on January 14, 1994.

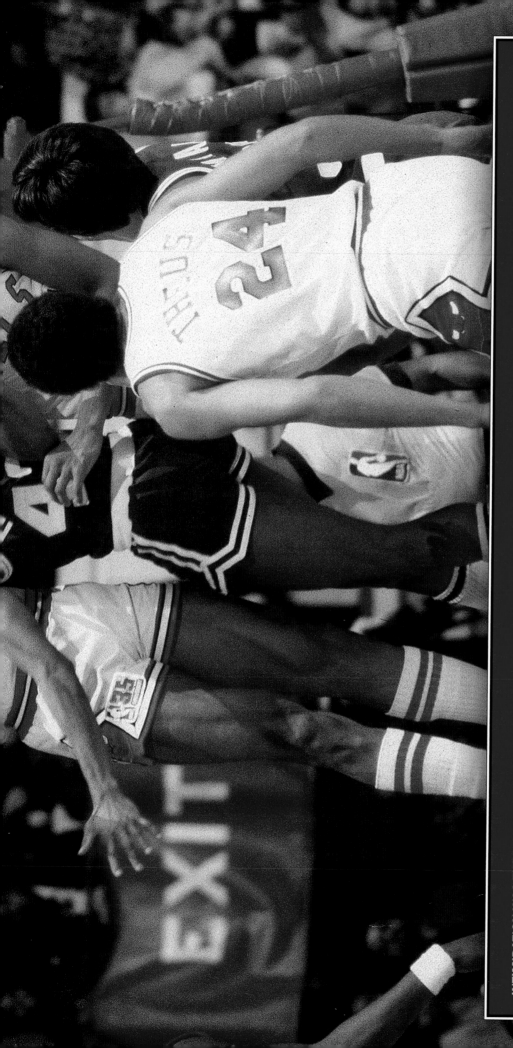

INTIMIDATION WAS THE NAME OF THE GAME FOR "THE A-TRAIN." Regarded as one of the strongest players ever to grace the court, Artis Gilmore made opposing players think twice before driving the lane. But off the court, Gilmore projected a low-key and quiet image, which made him one of the league's most distinctive personalities. It also made his few public statements

more powerful and intense. "Every time I walk out on the court, I plan to win," Gilmore said. "When I go on the court, I feel I should get every jump ball. At a certain point I have a feeling I have to get the ball." Gilmore started his career with the Kentucky Colonels of the American Basketball Association (ABA) and carried them to the playoffs in each of his five seasons

there. When the ABA folded, the Bulls chose Gilmore with the first pick in the dispersal draft. Unfortunately, his stint in Chicago produced unremarkable team results. But it wasn't for a lack of trying. The A-Train barreled along, racking up the highest career field-goal percentage in both the ABA (.557) and the NBA (.599).

CHAPTER TWO

AIR APPARENT

A new era began in 1984 when Chicago White Sox owner Jerry Reinsdorf began negotiations to purchase the Bulls. George Steinbrenner, principal owner of the New York Yankees, was also a part owner of the Bulls at the time. By chance, Steinbrenner mentioned to Reinsdorf that he was embarrassed by the Bulls and wanted to sell his stake. So a deal was quickly put together that allowed Reinsdorf to acquire more than half the team's stock, and he became the team's chairman in March 1985. The Bulls were coming off 4 consecutive losing seasons and averaging little more than 6,300 fans per game at Chicago Stadium. But Reinsdorf was determined to put a winner on the floor, and the team had a great player around whom it could rebuild—a dynamic rookie shooting guard named Michael Jordan.

A Chicago native, center Dave Corzine gave the Bulls steady work on the boards during some unremarkable seasons in the early 1980s.

MICHAEL JORDAN BECAME ONE OF THE GREAT-
EST PLAYERS OF ALL TIME BECAUSE HE NEVER
STOPPED PRACTICING. He also believed that his
pregame rituals contributed to his success. From his
days playing against his older brother Larry to his
private practices as a pro, Jordan was always trying
to improve. Once he became famous, though, finding

time to practice on his own became nearly impossible.
So Jordan would arrive at Chicago Stadium before
anyone else. As game time approached, he would put
on his baby-blue University of North Carolina shorts
underneath his Bulls shorts, get his ankles taped, and
put on a new pair of shoes. Then, just before tip-off, he
would apply resin to his hands, walk over to Bulls color

commentator Johnny Kerr, and clap his hands in front
of Kerr's face, creating a cloud of dust. It was a playful
action, but for Jordan, it became an important part of his
routine. Appropriately, when Jordan retired, Kerr walked
up to him with resin on his hands and slapped them
together in front of Jordan's face. "You got me," Jordan
said with a big grin.

ordan sent shockwaves throughout the league as soon as he joined

Chicago as the third overall pick in the 1984 NBA Draft. With

unstoppable moves, explosive quickness, and unrivaled leaping

ability, "Air" Jordan soared to dizzying heights, leading the Bulls in every

major statistical category. He was the runaway choice as 1985 NBA

Rookie of the Year and became an instant All-Star. But still, Chicago

remained a losing team.

In Jordan's second season, he missed 64 games with a broken foot.

The team urged him to sit out the remaining games, but after Jordan

accused management of not wanting to make the playoffs so the Bulls

could obtain a better draft pick, he was reluctantly allowed to return. With

just 15 games to go in the regular season, he worked alongside rugged

forward Charles Oakley to carry the Bulls into the playoffs. Although they

were swept by the Boston Celtics in three games, Jordan established

himself as a major force in Game 2 by scoring an NBA playoff-record

63 points. His performance was so miraculous that Celtics forward Larry

Bird commented, "It must be God disguised as Michael Jordan."

The 1986–87 season signaled a major turning point for the Bulls'

fortunes. The team solidified its coaching regime with the talented but

untested Doug Collins, and general manager Jerry Krause was deter-

mined to get Jordan some help. So in the 1987 NBA Draft, Chicago se-

lected forward Horace Grant and traded for little-known forward Scottie Pippen from the University of Central Arkansas. "I never heard of him or his school," Jordan at first said of Pippen. But the rookie's skills quickly opened Jordan's eyes. Behind the unstoppable duo of Jordan and Pippen, Chicago became a powerhouse in the Eastern Conference and won 50 games that season.

However, Chicago's quest for a championship was thwarted by the rough-and-tumble Detroit Pistons in the second round of the 1988 playoffs. Detroit coach Chuck Daly and his All-Star cast of "Bad Boys," such as center Bill Laimbeer and forward Dennis Rodman, developed "The Jordan Rules," a strategy for containing Jordan. They felt that Jordan's superstar status led referees to give him preferential treatment over opposing guards, so the Pistons got physical with Jordan and tried to throw him off balance with different defensive formations and hard fouls. "You hear about [The Jordan Rules] often enough—and

the referees hear it, too—and you start to think they have something different," said Chicago assistant coach John Bach. "It has an effect, and suddenly people think they aren't fouling Michael, even when they are."

After adding veteran center Bill Cartwright and shooting guard Craig Hodges before the 1988–89 season, the Bulls finished near the bottom of the Central Division but defeated the Cleveland Cavaliers in the first round of the playoffs. Jordan, now playing point guard, had promised that the Bulls would win the Cleveland series, and he contributed to the effort with averages of 39.8 points, 8.2 assists, and 5.8 rebounds in 5 games. With time about to expire in Game 5, he drove to his left at the top of the key and hit a hanging jumper to give the Bulls a one-point victory. "[Jordan] is the greatest competitor I've ever seen," Bach said afterwards, "and then he goes to still another level in the big games." But once again, it was all for naught. Although Chicago went on to beat the Knicks in the second round, the Pistons eliminated the Bulls in six games in the Eastern Conference finals.

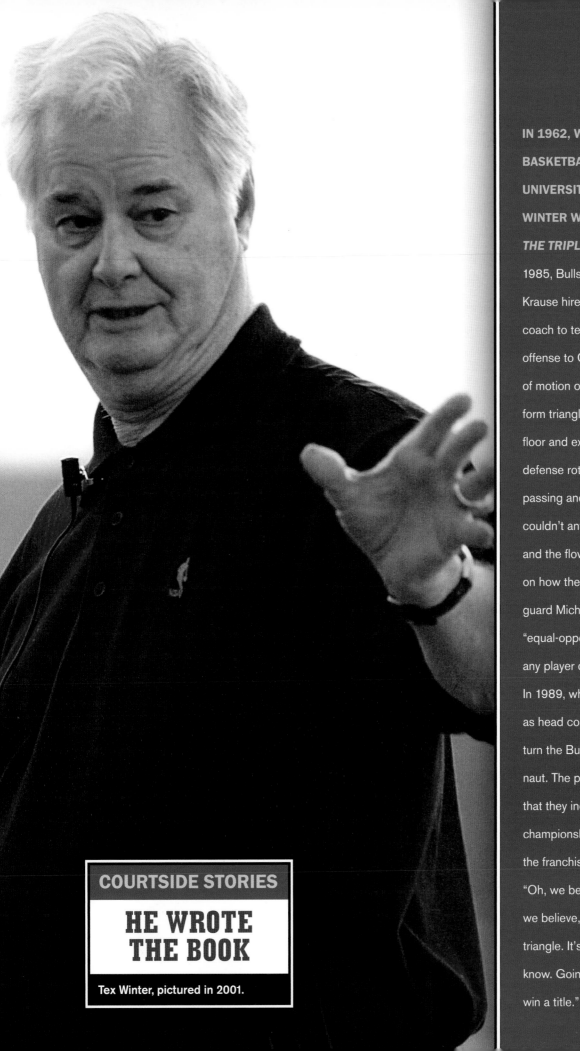

HE WROTE THE BOOK

Tex Winter, pictured in 2001.

IN 1962, WHILE COACHING BASKETBALL AT KANSAS STATE UNIVERSITY, MORICE "TEX" WINTER WROTE A BOOK CALLED *THE TRIPLE-POST OFFENSE.* In 1985, Bulls general manager Jerry Krause hired Winter as an assistant coach to teach his so-called triangle offense to Chicago's players. This form of motion offense required players to form triangles on different parts of the floor and exchange positions as the defense rotated. It relied upon quick passing and few plays, so the defense couldn't anticipate player movement, and the flow of the offense depended on how the defense moved. Bulls guard Michael Jordan called it the "equal-opportunity offense" because any player could get open at any time. In 1989, when Phil Jackson took over as head coach, the triangle helped turn the Bulls into a scoring juggernaut. The players were so appreciative that they included lyrics about it in a championship rap written to celebrate the franchise's first NBA title in 1991: "Oh, we believe in the triangle, Tex, we believe, yeah, we believe in the triangle. It's the show for those in the know. Goin' to the triangle and goin' to win a title."

FOLLOWING TRUSTED MENTORS WAS A RECURRING THEME IN PHIL JACKSON'S BASKETBALL CAREER.

It began in the fifth grade in Great Falls, Montana, with "Babe," a coach who spent extra practice time teaching Jackson how to shoot a step hook. In the seventh grade, Jackson started to learn every position on the basketball court. That's when 4-H agent Don Hotchkiss, who started a six-county basketball league in Montana and North Dakota, discovered Jackson's skills. The 4-H slogan, "Learn by doing," would later help form Jackson's unique, Zen style of coaching. He kept things simple, from pregame pep talks such as "Do what you were prepared to do," to his adoption of NBA coach Red Holzman's game philosophy: hit the open man and quickly get back on defense. Eventually, one of his most effective methods of getting his message across became silence. Once, when the Bulls were lagging behind in points and not heeding his directions, Jackson called a timeout and stood silently staring at his players. "The message was pretty clear," assistant coach John Bach said. "You're not listening, so solve it yourself." By 2010, Jackson had won 11 NBA championships as coach: 6 with the Bulls and 5 with the Los Angeles Lakers.

The 1989–90 season was a momentous one. Collins was let go, and one of his assistants, Phil Jackson, was named head coach. The move proved to be an excellent one as the Bulls rolled up a regular-season record of 55–27, then charged back for a conference finals re-match with Detroit. It took seven games, but Detroit dispatched Chicago again en route to its second straight NBA championship.

Rising star Michael Jordan and the Bulls waged some epic playoff battles against the rough-and-tumble Pistons in the late 1980s.

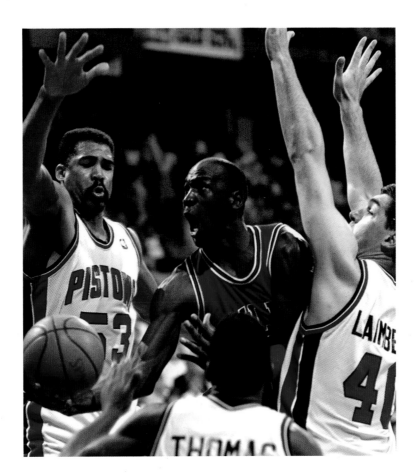

CHAPTER THREE

BULLISH DOMINATION

After numerous postseason losses—so many of which were to the Pistons—Coach Jackson convinced his team that although Jordan was its star, everyone needed to contribute if Chicago was going to succeed. So supporting players such as sharpshooter John Paxson and baby-faced guard B. J. Armstrong stepped up their efforts. And when the 1990–91 season opened, the Bulls were confident that their time had come.

Chicago reached the end of the regular season with a 61–21 record. In the second round of the playoffs against the Philadelphia 76ers, Jordan's performance was simply unbelievable, as he propelled Chicago to victory by averaging 43 points, 7.4 assists, and 6.6 rebounds per game. Lying in wait was Detroit, Chicago's old nemesis, but this time, the Bulls were not intimidated and proved it by dispatching the Pistons in a four-game sweep. "They got in our head with the physical stuff," admitted Pippen. "But in doing it, the Pistons taught us the toughness we needed."

Known for both his youthful appearance and his precise shooting touch, B. J. Armstrong wore Chicago red and black for seven seasons.

BY THE 1992–93 SEASON, PHOENIX SUNS FORWARD ED NEALY WAS 32 YEARS OLD, AND SUNS COACH COTTON FITZSIMMONS WAS HARD-PRESSED TO FIND A PLACE FOR HIM. But Fitzsimmons, who had drafted Nealy in 1982 when both were with the Kansas City Kings, had vowed to keep him in the NBA as long as possible. The Bulls agreed to take Nealy on as their 12th man in 1993, and as it turned out, Nealy's understated personality and exemplary work ethic had a positive influence on the Bulls as they wrapped up their "three-peat" season. He was always the first one at practice. He never complained when he didn't play, and he rarely took a shot when he did. He set screens, boxed out opponents, and always took on the other team's strongest player. Because Nealy did the dirty work so well, star guard Michael Jordan knew he could always depend on the forward during the few minutes he played. "He's the only one who'll set a good pick," Jordan declared. "He's a tough guy." That toughness endeared him to the hardworking Bulls fans who saw something of themselves in Nealy's blue-collar play that season.

COURTSIDE STORIES

A CHICAGO KIND OF PLAYER

Ed Nealy looks to move the ball.

Chicago so frustrated the Pistons that many of Detroit's stars walked off the court in the final game before the last seconds had even ticked off the clock. The Bulls then advanced to the long-elusive NBA Finals, where they faced the Lakers.

The Lakers and star guard Magic Johnson surprised the Bulls by winning the first game, but Chicago took the next four straight. In doing so, the team proved Jackson's theory correct—although Jordan confirmed his superstar status, it was his strong supporting cast that helped Chicago win its first-ever NBA championship. The critics had said Jordan was the phenom who couldn't win a title. Now, not only had he and his team won, but he had done it in the way he had always dreamed: as the Finals' Most Valuable Player (MVP). Jordan was chosen unanimously, and 1 of the 11 electors even tried to refuse the ballot, saying, "Who else could it be?" The morning after that final victory, Jordan couldn't put the championship trophy down, and he slept with it all the way from Los Angeles back to Chicago.

Chicago's wait would not be so long for the second title. The next season, the Bulls rumbled to a team-record 67–15 mark, breezed through

SCOTTIE PIPPEN'S CAREER WAS MARKED BY BOTH
FORTUNE AND MISFORTUNE. Fortune, because Bulls
general manager Jerry Krause so believed in the little-
known player's abilities that he traded for the rights to
draft "Pip," which allowed Pippen to win six NBA titles.
Misfortune, because he played on the same team as
Michael Jordan, who was considered by many to be the

best basketball player ever, making Pippen something
of an afterthought. But according to center Bill Wennington, a Bulls teammate, one need not look farther
than Chicago's first season after Jordan retired for proof
of Pippen's value. Pippen emerged as the leader of the
Bulls in 1993–94 and displayed the true measure of
his abilities. "Scottie Pippen led the team to 55 wins,

and only 1 bad call in a playoff game in New York kept
us from going to the NBA Finals," Wennington noted.
"He did it without Michael, going further without Michael
than Michael ever did without Scottie. Maybe it's apples
and oranges, but that season was an indication of what
Scottie was capable of doing as a team leader."

the playoffs, and throttled the Portland Trail Blazers in six games in the NBA Finals. The Bulls then "three-peated" in 1993 by beating star forward Charles Barkley and the Phoenix Suns in six games, thanks in part to some sharp three-point shooting by veteran guard Trent Tucker. Then Jordan, who was at the top of his game with nothing more to prove, suddenly decided to retire—a decision prompted in part by the murder of his father, James, in a 1993 robbery. At age 30, the NBA's best player walked away to pursue a career in professional baseball.

With Pippen now leading the way, the Bulls won more games than they lost in the next two seasons, but their horns were dulled without the presence of their star. Jordan, too, was feeling down. Although he was improving as a baseball player for the minor league Birmingham (Alabama) Barons, his dream of making the major leagues looked dim.

MICHAEL AND MARS

Michael Jordan's original 1985 model "Air Jordan" shoes.

IN THE EARLY 1990S, MICHAEL JORDAN'S SENSATIONAL STYLE OF PLAY MADE HIM ONE OF THE MOST FAMOUS PEOPLE IN THE WORLD. Another element of Jordan's fame was his participation in advertisements for Nike's "Air Jordan" basketball shoes. As Nike chairman Phil Knight explained in 1992, Jordan's image made the shoes into a status symbol. "Not every player has the style of Michael Jordan, and if we tried to make 'Air Jordan' appeal to everyone, it would lose its meaning," Knight said. "We had to slice up basketball itself." The black-and-white "Air Jordan" commercials featured Jordan with Mars Blackmon, an alter ego for filmmaker Spike Lee, who got his point across by using repetition to explain how great a player Jordan was. In one commercial, Blackmon said: "Nobody in the world can cover my main man, Michael Jordan. Nobody, nobody, nobody." Jordan, who had been dunking baskets in the background, then came over to cover Blackmon's mouth. These brief and humorous commercials, seen by a wide television audience, further increased Jordan's celebrity status outside of basketball.

n August 1994, Chicago opened the United Center, a new arena that would house both the Bulls and the National Hockey League's Blackhawks. With its exterior designed to look like old Chicago Stadium, it became known as "The House that Jordan Built" and featured a statue of the Hall-of-Famer out front. And several months after its opening, Jordan returned home to suit up once more. He elected to wear jersey number 45, since his former number, 23, had already been retired by the team. In the 1995 playoffs, Jordan and the Bulls fell to the Orlando Magic. Afterwards, Orlando guard Nick Anderson told reporters that the new Jordan wasn't equal to the old. "That number 45, he isn't Superman," Anderson said. "Number 23 was, but this guy isn't."

Stung by that loss, Jordan took his old jersey number out of retirement. The Bulls then added Dennis Rodman, a heavily tattooed forward known for his energetic rebounding skills, to the lineup. In 1995–96, Chicago's 72–10 regular-season mark set a new NBA record for most wins in a season. The Bulls then proved unstoppable in the playoffs, charging to their fourth NBA championship in six years by defeating the Seattle SuperSonics in the Finals. "This means a lot to me," said an emotional Jordan. "People doubted us. We proved them wrong."

Dennis Rodman was one of the NBA's great oddities, compensating for poor offensive skills with ferocious rebounding and defense.

Over the next two seasons, no one doubted the Bulls as they stampeded to two more NBA championships. Jackson's thoughtful coaching and a scrappy supporting cast that included center Luc Longley, guard Steve Kerr, and Croatian forward Toni Kukoc kept the Bulls rolling. In Game 6 of the 1998 NBA Finals—his last game in a Bulls uniform—Jordan poured in 45 points, including the game-winning basket, to top the Jazz for the Bulls' sixth championship in eight years.

After a 13-season career in which he won 5 NBA MVP awards and 6 NBA Finals MVP awards and completely rewrote Chicago's record books, Jordan again retired from the Bulls. Shortly after that, Pippen was traded away, Rodman was released, and Coach Jackson left the team to join the Lakers. One of the greatest dynasties in NBA history had ended.

An import from Croatia, Toni Kukoc was a pioneer of sorts, helping pave the way for a new generation of European stars to join the NBA.

CHAPTER FOUR

THE BABY BULLS

Forced to rebuild for the 1998–99 season, the Bulls traded away Longley and Kerr to make way for new players. Only Kukoc and guard Ron Harper returned as starters from the previous year's championship team. Chicago also hired former college coach Tim Floyd as its new head man. The new-look Bulls struggled. Their streak of home-game sellouts ended at 610 games in 2000, and Floyd resigned in 2001. Former Bulls center Bill Cartwright took over as coach for the remainder of that season and 2002–03, but he was also unsuccessful at turning the franchise's fortunes around.

Things seemed to spiral to new depths when the Bulls' top pick in the 2002 NBA Draft, standout point guard Jay Williams, played just one promising season before a motorcycle accident left the 21-year-old with career-ending leg and pelvis injuries. Making matters worse, the Bulls made several questionable trades and management decisions. So soon after being a coveted destination for NBA players, Chicago suddenly became

Ron Harper was an elite scorer in his first eight NBA seasons, but after joining Chicago in 1994, he reinvented himself as a star defender.

an unattractive place to play. It got so bad that even Jordan—the greatest Bulls player of all time—spurned Chicago in 2001, electing instead to play for the Washington Wizards during a two-year comeback stint. And while Pippen did return for one last season in 2003–04, he was limited to just 23 games due to injuries.

Things finally started to come together in 2004 under coach Scott Skiles, a former NBA point guard known for his heart and hustle. Before the 2004–05 season, most experts predicted that the Bulls would continue to struggle. The team, now led by rookie point guard Ben Gordon, actually started the season worse than expected, losing its first nine games. But then something happened that Chicagoans hadn't seen in eight long years—the team started playing together … and winning!

HOME-COURT ADVANTAGE

Joakim Noah tries to protect the rim during a game in the United Center.

MANY PROFESSIONAL BASKETBALL TEAMS HAVE GONE TO GREAT LENGTHS TO GAIN A HOME-COURT ADVANTAGE. The floor of the Celtics' old Boston Garden had hollow spots that made dribbling a challenge. The Milwaukee Bucks' tight nets gave their players extra time to get back on defense after a made basket. But Chicago's United Center, which opened in 1994, was built with more than one interesting advantage. First were the notoriously stiff rims, which lowered the shooting percentages of visiting teams—and even the Bulls themselves. Second, the spectator stands were located farther away from the court than normal, so a shooter's depth perception was altered, and some of the lights were positioned so as to play even more visual tricks. Finally, the building's temperature was often colder than most NBA stadiums. "This is a building you don't shoot well in," Bulls coach Phil Jackson once said. "It's the backboards, the basket standards, the rim, and the ambience and the surrounding environs that make it not a shooter's place. It's just a variety of things, but we try not to psychologically be intimidated by it."

THE BULLS HAVE ALWAYS TRIED TO MAKE GAME NIGHT INTERESTING— AND THEMATIC—FOR THE FANS.

They have a mascot named Benny the Bull, the Luvabulls cheerleading team, the Stampede Drumline, and even the Junior Luvabulls and Swingin' Seniors (dance teams made up of young girls and senior citizens). And in September 2003, after just a few rehearsals, the Matadors appeared on national television shows on a whirlwind media blitz before they debuted in person on November 7. That's when United Center public address announcer Steve Scott introduced Chicago to its newest team of cheerleaders: "The hype is for real and the time has come. … Please, welcome to the floor your very own … MATADORS!" Everything about the Matadors is big—their size, their enthusiasm, and their pride in the Bulls. The only mission of these 12 men is to make people laugh. Unlike other cheerleaders, a Matador need not be physically fit, have dance experience, nor a sense of shame. Each Matador is dressed in his own outrageous outfit, from bull horns and boxer shorts to capes and body paint.

COURTSIDE STORIES

THE MATADORS

The Matadors in action in 2009.

With a roster of players who averaged 25 years of age, Chicago's team became known as "The Baby Bulls," and developing stars such as guard Kirk Hinrich helped the Baby Bulls mature. More importantly, big men Eddy Curry and Tyson Chandler, centers who had been drafted straight out of high school in 2001 and had taken longer than expected to learn the NBA ropes, were showing signs of greatness. Several talented rookies, including point guard Chris Duhon and forward Luol Deng, also emerged as major contributors. "They are good," Skiles said of his rookies. "You are never really sure what you are going to get even though they played big games in college." For the first time since the '90s dynasty left town, the Bulls achieved a winning record and made the playoffs. Although the team lost in the first round of the 2005 postseason, Chicago seemed to have regained traction at last.

After battling to a 41–41 record in 2005–06 and returning to the playoffs only to be eliminated again in the first round, Chicago signed tough center Ben Wallace away from rival Detroit before the 2006–07 season. The Bulls now featured a solid, hardworking mix of youth and veterans who swept the defending NBA champion Miami Heat in the first round of the 2007 playoffs. Even though they were then eliminated by Detroit four games to two, the Bulls were making some noise again.

The 2007–08 season was a major step backwards that ended 33–49, but new head coach Vinny Del Negro took over in 2008 and promptly took his young squad—led by the dependable Gordon, explosive rookie point guard Derrick Rose, and high-energy center Joakim Noah—to a playoff berth with a 41–41 mark. Chicago made the most of its seven nail-biting postseason games in 2009, forcing the defending NBA champion Celtics into overtime in four of the contests—a first for an NBA playoff series—before ultimately losing the thrilling series. The Bulls then assembled a near-duplicate season in 2009–10, going 41–41 again before suffering another first-round postseason knockout, this time at the hands of superstar forward LeBron James and the Cavaliers.

From the early days of Sloan and the A-Train to the unstoppable Jordan dynasty, the Chicago Bulls have always been a proud franchise. Like the hardworking city of Chicago itself, they never give in, and they always strive to reach new heights. That determined template remains intact as today's Bulls lineup hopes to make some new championship memories for fans in the Windy City.

Ben Gordon (opposite) departed the Windy City in 2009, but Bulls fans continued to cheer the promising tandem of forward Joakim Noah and guard Derrick Rose (pictured, left to right, pages 46–47).

INDEX